ISBN 978-0-259-42058-3
PIBN 10816536

English
Français
Deutsche
Italiano
Español
Português

www.forgottenbooks.com

Mythology Photography **Fiction**
Fishing Christianity **Art** Cooking
Essays Buddhism Freemasonry
Medicine **Biology** Music **Ancient
Egypt** Evolution Carpentry Physics
Dance Geology **Mathematics** Fitness
Shakespeare **Folklore** Yoga Marketing
Confidence Immortality Biographies
Poetry **Psychology** Witchcraft
Electronics Chemistry History **Law**
Accounting **Philosophy** Anthropology
Alchemy Drama Quantum Mechanics
Atheism Sexual Health **Ancient History**
Entrepreneurship Languages Sport
Paleontology Needlework Islam
Metaphysics Investment Archaeology
Parenting Statistics Criminology
Motivational

OF THE

Angel Warriors
at Mons,

DURING THE RETREAT:

AND THE

Apparitions at the Battles
of the
Marne and Aisne,

With a Resumé of
Ancient and Modern Celestial Interventions
and
Parallel Instances from Scripture and other Reliable Sources.

By
·JOHN J. PEARSON,
Sometime Editor of the "INDIAN HERALD" and "KARACHI BEACON."

THE RATIONALE
OF THE
Angel Warriors
at Mons,
DURING THE RETREAT;
AND THE
Apparitions at the Battles
OF THE
Marne and Aisne,

WITH A Résumé OF
Ancient and Modern Celestial Interpositions
AND
Popular Instances from Scripture and other Reliable Sources.

By

JOHN J. PEARSON,
Sometime Editor of the "INDIAN HERALD" and "KARACHI BEACON."

Price 2d.

LONDON
CHRISTIAN GLOBE CO., Ltd., Fleet Street, E.C.

THE RATIONALE

OF THE

Angel Warriors at Mons

DURING THE RETREAT:

AND THE

APPARITIONS AT THE BATTLES
OF THE MARNE AND AISNE.

With a Resumé

OF ANCIENT AND MODERN CELESTIAL
INTERVENTIONS AND PARALLEL
INSTANCES FROM RELIABLE SOURCES.

By

JOHN J. PEARSON,

Sometime Editor of the
"Herald" and "Karachi Beacon."

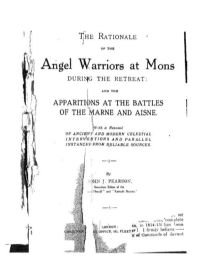

LONDON:
CHRISTIAN HERALD OFFICE, 145, FLEET ST.

THE RATIONALE

OF THE

Angel Warriors at Mons

DURING THE RETREAT:

AND THE

APPARITIONS AT THE BATTLES
OF THE MARNE AND AISNE.

With a Resumé

OF ANCIENT AND MODERN CELESTIAL
INTERVENTIONS AND PARALLEL
INSTANCES FROM RELIABLE SOURCES.

By

JOHN J. PEARSON,

Sometime Editor of the
"Herald" and "Karachi Beacon."

LONDON:
CHRISTIAN HERALD OFFICE, 183, FLEET ST.

(or
&a, in 1814-15) has been
I firmly believe ——
of thousands of devout

FOREWORD.

THE entire country has been much exercised by stories of Angelic Intervention on behalf of the Allies at and during the Retreat from Mons, and in the tremendous conflicts on the Marne and Aisne, whereby the German hosts were hurled back, just as it appeared Paris was about to fall into their hands. Humanly speaking, no earthly power could have arrested the Teutonic flood that swept through Belgium and over North-Eastern France ; and it seemed to those of us who remembered the Campaigns of 1870, that history would again repeat itself, and that the whole of Northern France and the Capital would have quickly succumbed to the might of the German Power.

The idea of the Military Chiefs of the Fatherland was to make a rush for Paris, under the impression that, having once obtained possession of the French Capital, the subjugation of the rest of the country would be a task easy of accomplishment. Half a century ago, this conception might have had some foundation in fact, for of a truth Paris was then France, and France was Paris. But our neighbours across the silver streak have learned wisdom since the fatal war of 45 years ago : and even if Paris had fallen into the hands of the German hordes, France would have fought on to the bitter end. By a merciful interposition of Providence, the first and principal design of that upstart and ambitious Power (whose Capital Berlin has been the storm-centre of Europe for upward of 170 years, and which was only rescued from complete annihilation by Great Britain and Russia, in 1814-15) has been frustrated ; *but not merely by human power !* I firmly believe —— and I think that I am voicing the opinion of thousands of devout

FOREWORD.

THE entire country has been much exercised by stories of Angelic Intervention on behalf of the Allies at and during the Retreat from Mons, and in the tremendous conflicts on the Marne and Aisne, whereby the German hosts were hurled back, just as it appeared Paris was about to fall into their hands. Humanly speaking, no earthly power could have arrested the Teutonic flood that swept through Belgium and over North-Eastern France; and it seemed to those of us who remembered the Campaigns of 1870, that history would again repeat itself, and that the whole of Northern France and the Capital would have quickly succumbed to the might of the German Power.

The idea of the Military Chiefs of the Fatherland was to make a rush for Paris, under the impression that, having once obtained possession of the French Capital, the subjugation of the rest of the country would be a task easy of accomplishment. Half a century ago, this conception might have had some foundation in fact, for of a truth Paris was then France, and France was Paris. But our neighbours across the silver streak have learned wisdom since the fatal war of 45 years ago: and even if Paris had fallen into the hands of the German hordes, France would have fought on to the bitter end. By a merciful interposition of Providence, the first and principal design of that upstart and ambitious Power (whose Capital Berlin has been the storm-centre of Europe for upward of 170 years, and which was only rescued from complete annihilation by Great Britain and Russia, in 1814-15) has been frustrated; *but not merely by human power!* I firmly believe —— and I think that I am voicing the opinion of thousands of devout readers, because I am satisfied that the opinions herein expressed, if seriously regarded, cannot fail to produce in all of us " The fruits of good living," and make us far wiser and happier in the great future that lies before us.

ANCIENT BELIEFS.

With most people, who in Western Europe are spoken of as learned," the ancient Greeks and Romans are regarded as having been the pioneers of all human thought and invention, while the great masters of China, India, Chaldea, Egypt, and Phœnicia, to whom the Greco-Latin nations stood indebted for their language, alphabet, ideas, and religion, are neglected and forgotten! Classic scholars are aware that the Greeks and Romans entertained certain ideas regarding the State of the Soul, after the death of the body, which are now held to be purely mythical. Many of them, undoubtedly, are so; and of these I am not about to speak. But amongst their other conceits, there are some which, as they coincide with the plain teachings of Scripture, and the opinions of many of the most enlightened persons in this darkened period of the world's history, it is desirable to consider more closely. Amongst these conceptions, their belief in the Tripartate Kingdom of the Dead was very prominent. According to this belief, there were the Elysian Fields, a region in which a certain variety of happiness, chiefly of a gross and sensual nature, was enjoyed; and Tartarus, the place of punishment for the reprobate wicked; each of which was, comparatively, but sparsely inhabited by persons whose doom, was irrevocably fixed and settled for all eternity. But betwixt these two kingdoms, there was a third or mid-region peopled with vast hosts of wandering disembodied spirits, fully cognisant of everything done on earth, longing once more to take part in the concerns of this life, and pining to assist the People and Causes to which they were attached when in the flesh. And these souls, to whom old habits and pursuits were dear, and who could not break the links that bound them to the earth, were permitted again to " visit the glimpses of the moon," and, under the command of their old Chiefs and Heroes, take part in any special crisis affecting their kindred's or country's welfare.

The ancient literature of Southern and Western Asia teems with such celestial interferences in times of national stress; and so fixed is the idea in the Oriental mind, that to dispute it would be regarded as being at once impious and ridiculous. Although we

Readers, because I am satisfied that the opinions herein expressed, if seriously regarded, cannot fail to produce in all of us "the fruits of good living," and make us far wiser and happier in the great future that lies before us.

ANCIENT BELIEFS

With most people, who in Western Europe are spoken of as learned," the ancient Greeks and Romans are regarded as having been the pioneers of all human thought and invention, while the great masters of China, India, Chaldea, Egypt, and Phœnicia, to whom the Græco-Latin nations stood indebted for their language, alphabet, ideas, and religion, are neglected and forgotten. Classic scholars are aware that the Greeks and Romans entertained certain ideas regarding the State of the Soul, after the death of the body, which are now held to be purely mythical. Many of them, undoubtedly, are so; and of these I am not about to speak. But amongst their other conceits, there are some which, as they coincide with the plain teachings of Scripture, and the opinions of many of the most enlightened persons in this darkened period of the world's history, it is desirable to consider more closely. Amongst these conceptions, their belief in the Tripartate Kingdom of the Dead was very prominent. According to this belief, there were the Elysian Fields, a region in which a certain variety of happiness, chiefly of a gross and sensual nature, was enjoyed; and, Tartarus, the place of punishment for the reprobate wicked; each of which was, comparatively, but sparsely inhabited by persons whose doom was irrevocably fixed and settled for all eternity. But betwixt these two kingdoms, there was a third or mid region, peopled with vast hosts of wandering disembodied spirits, fully cognisant of everything done on earth, longing once more to take part in the concerns of this life, and pining to assist the People and Causes to which they were attached when in the flesh. And these souls, to whom old habits and pursuits were dear, and who could not break the links that bound them to the earth, were permitted again to "visit the glimpses of the moon;" and, under the command of their old Chiefs and Heroes, take part in any special crisis affecting their kindred's or country's welfare.

The ancient literature of Southern and Western Asia teems with such celestial interferences in times of national stress; and so fixed is the idea in the Oriental mind, that to gainsay it would be regarded as being at once impious and ridiculous. Although we cannot believe for a moment the old Turanian and Indian accounts of legions of angels and demons mingling in the battles of prehistoric day, nor the legends of the actions of the gods in the Trojan War; the prowess of Pollux and Castor at the Battle of Lake Regillus (noted in Macauley's Lays of Ancient Rome); the mingling of angelic warriors in the battles of the Crusaders, or those of the Peninsular between the Spaniards and Moors ; *for the simple reason that the interests of God's people (Israel) were not involved in these contests !* yet, as Dr. Johnson observed, " All history is for such manifestations : all reason against them." And as Lord ·Nugent remarked on the remarkable appearances" just *after* the Battle of Edge Hill, " That the world abounds with histories of preter" natural appearances, the most utterly incredible, but supported by testimonies the most undeniable," we are compelled, in common fairness to our fellowmen, to pause before rejecting these accounts as fabulous, and casting behind our backs the unanimous verdict of all history. Nay, it may be worth while to consider whether the opinions of the Ancient World, in regard to the Interposition of Unearthly Beings in mundane affairs, may have some foundation in fact __ whether such might not be remnants of tradition handed down from the earliest inhabitants of the earth, or wrested from Nature by long observation, if not, indeed, communicated to man from a higher source. And whether circumstances of constant recurrence in all Ages and in all Regions, frequently observed and recorded by persons utterly ignorant of all history but that of their own times, and unacquainted with the dogmas of any creed but their own, do not (as well as various passages in Holy Writ), afford a striking confirmation of this theory of supernal interference in the affairs of mankind : whilst, on the other hand it affords a natural, convenient, and satisfactory explanation of their seeming mystery.

"CREDAT ·JUDAEÜS ¨APELLA."

I will here reproduce one or two thoughts expressed in one of the Articles on " The Fulfilment of Holy Writ," now appearing every week in the columns of the *Christian Globe*, as bearing on the subject we are now discussing.

" To minds which can admit nothing but what can be explained and demonstrated on mathematical and physical grounds, a consideration of anything savouring of the supernatural must appear perfectly idle : for while the most acute intellect or the most powerful

logic can throw but little light on the subject, it is, at the same time (though I entertain a confident hope that this will not always be the case) equally irreducible within the bounds of science. Meanwhile, experience, observation, intuition, and, above all, the teachings of the Book of Books, must be our principal. If not, indeed, our only guides. Because in the Seventeenth Century, owing to certain reason, discretion, and the warranty of Scripture, the Eighteenth Century, by a natural reaction, sank into the opposite extreme of apathy, to be followed by the censorious criticism and credulity of the past century, and the blasphemous atheism and contemptuous scorn of to-day. But whoever closely observes the "Signs of the Times," must be aware that another change is impending, of which the mixed reception of the story of the " Angels at Mons" is highly suggestive. The superficious scepticism of the past and present age is yielding to a more humble and reverent spirit of inquiry : and there is a large and growing class of well informed people, amongst the most enlightened and unprejudiced of the present day, who are beginning to consider that much which they had been hitherto taught to reject as fabulous, has been, in reality, ill- or misunderstood truth.

Somewhat of the deep things regarding our own being, and of the mysteries by which we are surrounded, is looming upon us — as yet, it is true but darkly ; but I feel certain more light will shortly be vouchsafed to us, and we shall soon realise the full truth of Zechariah's prophecy, " It shall come to pass, that at evening time it shall be light " (Zech. xiv., 7). " Now we see through a glass darkly ; but then face to face ; now we know in part, but then shall we know even as also we are known." (1 Cor. xiii., 12). Soon, very soon, we shall have more striking manifestations of angelic intervention on our behalf, which will be too glaringly apparent either to be denied or explained away by man's obstinacy or the "oppositions of science, falsely so-called" (1 Tim. vi. 20). Mean while we must possess our souls in patience; and grope our way along the dim path before us, ever in danger of being led into error, from which we may escape by looking only to the "More sure word of prophecy ; whereunto we shall do well that we take heed, as unto a light that shineth in a dark place, until the day dawn, and the Day Star arise in our hearts." (2 Peter i., 19), while we may count on being pursued, if not by open persecution, by the " slings and arrows " of ridicule — that weapon so easy to wield, so potent against the weak, so impotent against the strong — which has often retarded the births of so many truths, but never thoroughly stifled one.

logic can throw but little light on the subject. It is, at the same time (though I entertain a confident hope that this will not always be the case) equally irreducible within the bounds of science. Meanwhile experience, observation, intuition, and, above all, the teachings of the Book of Books, must be our principal, if not, indeed, our only guides. Because in the Seventeenth Century, credulity ran riot; reason, discretion, and the warranty of Scripture the Eighteenth Century, by a natural reaction, sunk into the opposite extreme of apathy, to be followed by the censorious criticism and unbelief of the past century, and the blasphemous atheism and contemptuous scorn of to-day. But whoever closely observes the "Signs of the Times," must be aware that another change is impending, of which the mixed reception of the story of the "Angels of Mons" is highly suggestive. The superstitious scepticism of the past and present age is yielding to a more humble and reverent spirit of inquiry; and there is a large and growing class of well-informed people, amongst the most enlightened and unprejudiced of the present day, who are beginning to consider that much which they had been hitherto taught to reject as fabulous, has been, in reality, ill- or misunderstood truth."

Somewhat of the deep things regarding our own being, and of the mysteries by which we are surrounded, is looming upon us: as yet it is true but darkly; but I feel certain more light will shortly be vouchsafed to us, and we shall soon realize the full truth of Zechariah's prophecy, "It shall come to pass, that at evening time it shall be light" (Zech. xiv., 7). "Now we see through a glass darkly; but then face to face; now we know in part, but then shall we know even as also we are known." (1 Cor. xiii., 12). Soon, very soon, we shall have more striking manifestations of angelic intervention on our behalf; which will be too glaringly apparent either to be denied or explained away by man's obstinacy or the "oppositions of science, falsely so-called" (1 Tim. vi. 20). Meanwhile we must possess our souls in patience, and grope our way along the dim path before us, ever in danger of being led into error, from which we may escape by looking only to the "More sure word of prophecy; whereunto we shall do well that we take heed, as unto a light that shineth in a dark place, until the day dawn, and the Day Star arise in our hearts." (2 Peter i., 19); whilst we may count on being pursued, if not by open persecution, by the "slings and arrows" of ridicule——that weapon so easy to wield, so potent against the weak, so impotent against the strong——which has often retarded the births of so many truths, but never thoroughly stifled one.

"THE CAUSE WHICH I KNEW NOT I SEARCHED OUT."

(Job xxix., 16).

By investigation, I do not mean the hasty, carping, angry notice of an unwelcome fact, which too often arrogates the right of determining upon any question; but the cautious, modest, painstaking examination, that is content to wait for more light from the words of wisdom enshrined in the Word of God, and humbly follow out such disclosures, however opposed these may be to previously-formed theories, or mortifying to the pride of the human intellect. The pharisaic and scientific scepticism which at once denies without due investigation, is quite as dangerous, and much more contemptible than the ignorant and blind credulity which accepts, without thought or enquiry, anything and everything presented to it. It is, indeed, but another form of ignorance so frequently assuming to be knowledge.

Not a few scientific men have expressed their disbelief, *in toto*, of anything super-natural: but if certain scientific men could but comprehend how they discredit and belittle the science they profess to follow by their unbending scepticism and overweening confidence, they would certainly, for the sake of the science they affect to love, display more candour and liberality. And this reflection indeed naturally suggests another. Do they really love science for its own sake, or is it not with them but the *means* to an *end?* Does love of influence, of sordid greed of gain, or the estimation of their fellow-men ever sway their decisions? Were the love of true science more genuine, I rather suspect that we should see very different fruits from those we see borne by the tree of knowledge—as this flourishes at present. And this suspicion is strengthened by the recollection that amongst the numerous professors and students of the exact sciences I have at different times encountered in this and other countries, and during the course of a pretty active life, the real worshippers at the shrine of knowledge have all been men of the most simple, candid, unprejudiced, and enquiring minds; ever willing and ready to listen to every new suggestion, and investigate any new facts or theories presented to them, no matter by whom: not bold and self-sufficient, but humble and reverent students, who, aware of their own ignorance and unworthiness, and conscious that they are yet in the primer of Nature's works, do not allow themselves to pronounce hastily upon her disclosures, or set limits to her decrees.

The only way of attaining any glimpses of truth in a matter of which we know nothing whatever, where all *a priori* reasoning upon which is utterly valueless, and where our intellects can serve us so little, is to enter upon its investigation with the conviction that, knowing nothing, we are not entitled to reject any evidence that may be presented to us out of God's Word, or from the experience of others who have witnessed phenomena hidden from our eyes, but which is corroborated by other and independent witnesses. We must also pray for guidance: and ever remember that our puny intellects are no criterion or measure of God's Almighty Power or vast designs: and I think that one of the most irreverent, dangerous, and sinful things a man or woman can be guilty of, is to treat with scorn and derision, any information as to any phenomena, which, however strangely it may impress the mind, and however adverse it may be to our previously conceived opinions, may possibly be an intimation showing us the way to one of God's truths.

The belief in a Supreme Being, in supernal and infernal Spirits, and the inherent immortality of the Soul, is common to all nations and creeds: but our own unaided wisdom does not enable us to form any conception of any of these objects of faith. All the information open to us on these and kindred subjects is comprised in such lessons as the Holy Scripture here and there give us——and these only so far as illuminated and made comprehensible to us by their Divine Author——whatsoever other conclusions we draw must be the result either of our own intuition, our experience, or from observation. Unless founded upon these, the opinions of the most profound student of science, the most erudite theologian, or the most deeply read metaphysician that ever lived, are worth no more than those of any other person.

THE EVIDENCE AS TO THE ANGELS AT MONS AND ELSEWHERE.

The rumours as to the appearance of Celestial Warriors, and other unearthly phenomena, having been witnessed by large numbers of the Allied soldiery now engaged in fighting the Central European Powers (united in unholy alliance with the Turk) came simultaneously from both the Western and Eastern theatres of war, some time about the end of August last year (1914): and these must have been floating about in the ranks of the British, French,

"THE CAUSE WHICH I KNEW NOT I SEARCHED OUT."

(Job xxix., 16).

By investigation, I do not mean the hasty, carping, angry notice of an unwelcome fact, which too often arrogates the right of determining upon any question; but the cautious, modest, painstaking examination that is content to wait for more light from the words of wisdom enshrined in the Word of God, and humbly follow out such disclosures, however opposed these may be to previously-formed theories, or mortifying to the pride of the human intellect. The pharisaic and scientific scepticism which at once denies without due investigation, is quite as dangerous, and much more contemptible than the ignorant and blind credulity which accepts, without thought or enquiry, anything and everything presented to it. It is, indeed, but another form of ignorance so frequently assuming to be knowledge.

Not a few scientific men have expressed their disbelief, *in toto*, of anything super-natural: but if certain scientific men could but comprehend how they discredit and belittle the science they profess to follow by their unbending scepticism and overweening confidence, they would certainly, for the sake of the science they affect to love, display more candour and liberality. And this reflection indeed naturally suggests another. Do they really love science for its own sake, or is it not with them but the *means* to an *end*? Does love of influence, of sordid greed of gain, or the estimation of their fellow-men ever sway their decisions? Were the love of true science more genuine, I rather suspect that we should see very different fruits from those we see borne by the tree of knowledge—as this flourishes at present. And this suspicion is strengthened by the recollection that amongst the numerous professors and students of the exact sciences I have at different times encountered in this and other countries, and during the course of a pretty active life, the real worshippers at the shrine of knowledge have all been men of the most simple, candid, unprejudiced, and enquiring minds; ever willing and ready to listen to every new suggestion, and investigate any new facts or theories presented to them, no matter by whom: not bold and self-sufficient, but humble and reverent students, who, aware of their own ignorance and unworthiness, and conscious that they are yet in the primer of Nature's works, do not allow themselves to pronounce hastily upon her disclosures, or set limits to her decrees.

8

The only way of attaining any glimpses of truth in a matter of which we know nothing whatever, where all *a priori* reasoning upon which is utterly valueless, and where our intellects can serve us so little, is to enter upon its investigation with the conviction that, knowing nothing, we are not entitled to reject any evidence that may be presented to us out of God's Word, or from the experience of others who have witnessed phenomena hidden from our eyes, but which is corroborated by other and independent witnesses. We must also pray for guidance : and ever remember that our puny intellects are no criterion or measure of God's Almighty Power or vast designs : and I think that one of the most irreverent, dangerous, and sinful things a man or woman can be guilty of, is to treat with scorn and derision, any information as to any phenomena, which, however strangely it may impress the mind, may possibly be an intimation showing us the way to one of God's truths.

The belief in a Supreme Being, in supernal and infernal Spirits, and the inherent immortality of the Soul, is common to all nations and creeds : but our own unaided wisdom does not enable us to form any conception of any of these objects of faith. All the information open to us on these and kindred subjects is comprised in such lessons as the Holy Scripture here and there give us——and these only so far as illuminated and made comprehensible to us by their Divine Author——whatsoever other conclusions we draw must be the result either of our own intuition, our experience, or from observation. Unless founded upon these, the opinions of the most profound student of science, the most erudite theologian, or the most deeply read metaphysician that ever lived, are worth no more than those of any other person.

THE EVIDENCE AS TO THE ANGELS AT MONS AND ELSEWHERE.

The rumours as to the appearance of Celestial Warriors, and other unearthly phenomena, having been witnessed by large numbers of the Allied soldiery now engaged in fighting the Central European Powers (united in unholy alliance with the Turk) came simultaneously from both the Western and Eastern theatres of war, some time about the end of August last year (1914) : and these must have been floating about in the ranks of the British, French,

9

Russian, and Belgian Forces before they assumed the definite shape in which they now appear. To say that these stories originated in certain romantic tales published in a London Evening Journal is the veriest moonshine. For, in its edition of Saturday the 11th of September, 1915, the newspaper in question notifies that " *It will not be long before the story* (" The Bowman ") *is translated into nearly every European language, and not a few Eastern tongues.* It will thus be possible soon to read Mr. Machen's book in the following *seven languages :—English (including special American Edition), French, Italian, Russian, Danish, Norwegian, and Hindustani. Hitherto the Four Tales comprising the book have appeared in English only !* How comes it to pass that the stories of angelic warriors coming to the assistance of the troops ranged against Prussia, Austria, and the " unspeakable Turk," *were, and are rife amongst men who do not know one word of the English speech ?* And how was it that *these stories were bruited about for upwards of a month, throughout the camps, trenches, and hospitals* on both the Eastern and Western fronts of this terrible war ?

The Writer heard of them from the mouth of a fiercely fanatical German (now interned on board a vessel lying off Southend) who wildly informed me that the day was approaching when we (the British) would be called to strict account for using some strange and horrible devices, previously unknown in warfare, and by means of which thousands of his countrymen had been done to death, having been found dead without wound or scratch, or any other indication as to how they had come by their deaths. They had, the German Medical Staff decided, succumbed to some untraceable cause, and had not been killed in fair honest fight. He also averred that the British and French, had, by means of some terrifying spectral illusions, stampeded the horses of a Prussian Cavalry Corps, just as they were on the point of pressing home a successful charge upon our retreating troops: and that, as Germans were known as the most advanced chemists in the world, they would soon " give us a dose of our own physic," perhaps, stronger and more effective than ours had been. This was just after the commencement of the retreat from Mons, and *most certainly upwards of a full month before any story of these aerial phenomena appeared in any London Journal !* At the time, I regarded this outburst as being merely an explosion of German rancour on account of our having entered the lists as supporters of stricken Belgium, and outraged and insulted France and Russia. I have every reason now to think otherwise.

All the accounts——British, French, Belgium, and Russian,——

agree in two very important particulars, viz., that the Leader of these Angelic warriors was mounted on a *white* horse, and that He and His celestial followers were clad in glistening clothing. It matters not what the names bestowed on this Leader, by the many spectators of these visions——whether *St. George,* by the English, *St. Andrew,* by the Scots, *St. Patrick,* by the Irish, or *St. David,* by the Welsh, *St. Denis* or *Joan d'Arc* (who, be it remembered, always affected masculine garb, and for the resumption of which she was burnt to death in the market-place of Rouen, through the machinations of that very Church which has lately canonised her), by the French, *St. Michael,* by the Belgians, or *St. Nicholas* or *General Scobloff,* by the Russians——as the various beholders would naturally give Him the name that, from patriotism or religious training, was uppermost in their thoughts at the time. But whatever the appellation made use of, this cannot affect the identity of this Leader upon the *white* horse. Now turn to the Book of *Revelation,* in the New Testament (Chapter vi., 2 : and Chapter xix., 11-14), and it will be seen Who this Leader and His following really are. In both of these passages of Scripture, this Glorious Personage, and His attendants *are mounted on WHITE horses:* the former crowned, and most splendidly apparelled, and the latter garbed in " fine linen, white and clean." *And the Leader had a BOW !* " From these considerations (amongst others), I am convinced *that the phenomena witnessed by these men, of differing nationalities and creeds, during the Retreat from Mons, and the fierce actions on the Marne and Aisne were real and not imaginary.* And I am strongly inclined to think that it was a knowledge of the above facts—— *especially the accoutrement of the Great Central Figure*—— that suggested the title of " The Bowmen," rather than the reminiscence of the legendary story of St. George, and how he brought " his Agincourt *bowmen* to help the English !"

It is not very generally known that many of our monarchs, especially the first three Georges, affected *white* horses as chargers; and that the beautiful *white* Arab, Selim, was chosen by Napoleon the First, " the Man of Destiny "——who, had he had his will, would have left no upstart Prussia nor besotted Austria to trouble the peace of Europe and the world——under the influence of these very prophecies !

The number of combatants in the British, Oversea Dominions', French, Russian, and Belgian Armies who have deposed to the actual seeing of these aerial phenomena is very large ; and I do not propose to enter upon anything like a detailed description of any of these, as this has already been done in the various accounts

Russian, and Belgian Forces before they assumed the definite shape in which they now appear. To say that these stories originated in certain romantic tales published in a London Evening Journal is the veriest moonshine. For, in its edition of Saturday the 11th of September, 1915, the newspaper in question notifies that "*It will not be long before the story* (" The Bowman ") *is translated into nearly every European language, and not a few Eastern tongues.* It will thus be possible soon to read Mr. Machen's book in *the following seven languages :—English (including special American Edition), French, Italian, Russian, Danish, Norwegian, and Hindustani. Hitherto the Four Tales comprising the book have appeared in English only!* How comes it to pass that the stories of angelic warriors coming to the assistance of the troops ranged against Prussia, Austria, and the " unspeakable Turk," *were, and are rife amongst men who do not know one word of the English speech ?* And how was it that *these stories were bruited about for upwards of a month, throughout the camps, trenches, and hospitals* on both the Eastern and Western fronts of this terrible war?

The Writer heard them from the mouth of a fiercely fanatical German (now interned on board a vessel lying off Southend) who wildly informed me that the day was approaching when we (the British) would be called to strict account for using some strange and horrible devices, previously unknown in warfare, and by means of which thousands of his countrymen had been done to death, having been found dead without wound or scratch, or any other indication as to how they had come by their deaths. They had, the German Medical Staff decided, succumbed to some untraceable cause, and had not been killed in fair honest fight. He also averred that the British and French had, by means of some terrifying spectral illusions, stampeded the horses of a Prussian Cavalry Corps, just as they were on the point of pressing home a successful charge upon our retreating troops : and that, as Germans were known as the most advanced chemists in the world, they would soon "give us a dose of our own physic," perhaps, stronger and more effective than ours had been. This was just after the commencement of the retreat from Mons, and *most certainly upwards of a full month before any story of these aerial phenomena appeared in any London Journal !* At the time, I regarded this outburst as being merely an explosion of German rancour on account of our having entered the lists as supporters of stricken Belgium, and outraged and insulted France and Russia. I have every reason now to think otherwise.

All the accounts——British, French, Belgium, and Russian,——

10

agree in two very important particulars, *viz.*, that the Leader of these Angelic warriors was mounted on a *white* horse, and that He and His celestial followers were clad in glistening clothing. It matters not what the names bestowed on this Leader, by the many spectators of these visions——whether *St. George*, by the English, *St. Andrew*, by the Scots, *St. Patrick*, by the Irish, or *St. David*, by the Welsh, *St. Denis* or *Joan d'Arc* (who, be it remembered, always affected masculine garb, and for the resumption of which she was burnt to death in the market-place of Rouen, through the machinations of that very Church which has lately canonised her), by the French, *St Michael*, by the Belgians, or *St. Nicholas* or *General Scobeloff*, by the Russians——as the various beholders would naturally give Him the name that, from patriotism or religious training, was uppermost in their thoughts at the time. But whatever the appellation made use of, this cannot affect the identity of this Leader upon the *white* horse. Now turn to the Book of *Revelation*, in the New Testament (Chapter vi., 2 : and Chapter xix., 11-14), and it will be seen Who this Leader and His following really are. In both of these passages of Scripture, this Glorious Personage, and His attendants *are mounted on WHITE horses*: the Former crowned, and most splendidly apparelled, and the latter garbed in " fine linen, white and clean." *And the Leader had a BOW !* " From these considerations (amongst other), I am convinced *that the phenomena witnessed by these men, of differing nationalities and creeds, during the Retreat from Mons, and the fierce actions on the Marne and Aisne were real and not imaginary.* And I am strongly inclined to think that it was a knowledge of the above facts—— *especially the accoutrement of the Great Central Figure*—— that suggested the title of " The Bowmen," rather than the reminiscence of the legendary story of St. George, and how he brought " his Agincourt *bowmen* to help the English !"

It is not very generally known that many of our monarchs, especially the first three Georges, affected *white* horses as chargers ; and that the beautiful *white* Arab, Selim, was chosen by Napoleon the First, " the Man of Destiny "——who, had he had his will, would have left no upstart Prussia nor besotted Austria to trouble the peace of Europe and the world——under the influence of these very prophecies !

The number of combatants in the British, Oversea Dominions', French', Russian, and Belgian Armies who have deposed to the actual seeing of these aerial phenomena is very large ; and I do not propose to enter upon anything like a detailed description of any of these, as this has already been done in the various accounts

11

furnished by the newspapers, and in the many pamphlets now being published on this subject. These are merely so much sensational gossip, calculated to excite and feed the morbidly curious, without any attempt at any explanation of these remarkable occurrences. I will, however, remark, *en passant*, that if the stories published in the *Evening News* (*one month after these tales began to be noised about the camps on both the Eastern and Western fronts of the war*) and if they "*had no foundation in fact of any kind or sort*," but were spun out of the inner consciousness of their Author's brain, then I say that a more daring and wicked thing was never before attempted in the way of sensational journalism in this country. And this, in itself constitutes a glaring Sign of the fearful Times in which we are now living! "It is a snare to a man who devoureth that which is holy, and after vows to make enquiry." "Whoso boasteth himself of a false gift is like clouds and wind without rain. (Proverbs xx., 25 ; xxv., 14) : and it is a very dreadful thing to trifle with serious matters affecting the present welfare and the future destinies of mankind.

The number of persons in the British, French, Belgian, and Russian armies who have declared that they were eye-witnesses of these strange and unearthly manifestations, is, I have said, very great, and comprises men of every rank and temperament——from the highly-educated officer down to the humble, and often illiterate private. And it is safe to say that, under the fearful circumstances in which these men were placed——the horrors of a retreat (always depressing, and especially repugnant to British troops) before savage and vindictive enemies, employing barbarous and unheard of methods in the conduct of this war, and who were known, habitu-ally, and out of studied malice, to ignore all the customary usages of warfare ; the dreadful scenes of bloodshed, blazing towns, hamlets, and detached dwellings : the ruined and fleeing peasantry : the care of wounded and dying comrades; their own pitiable condition of fatigue, hunger, and privation, and the terrible state of the country throughout which they struggled under the precarious cover of rear-guard actions——*these heroic souls were not in a frame of mind conducive to the evolution of romantic thoughts or ideas on any subject whatever, much less in the concoction of deliberate falsehoods regarding subjects of a religious or spiritual nature* !

The *Universe* publishes a story told by an officer to the effect that he saw at the front an apparition of men armed with bows from which they discharged flights of arrows into the German host : and that afterwards, when talking to one of the German prisoners, the latter enquired as to the name of the officer mounted on a *white* horse who led the British, and gave it as his opinion that he must have borne a charmed life, for although he was such a conspicuous object, and hundreds were firing at him, none of them had been able to hit him !

A terribly wounded Lancashire Fusilier asked Miss Phyllis Campbell (who for some months acted as nurse at one of the Hospitals at the Front) for a medal or picture of St. George. Puzzled at the strange request, Miss Campbell inquired whether he was a Roman Catholic. "No," the man replied, "I am a Wesleyan Methodist, and I want a picture or a medal of St, George because I have seen him on a *white* horse, leading the British at Vitry-le-François, when the Allies turned upon the Germans." Seeing Miss Camp-bell's look of astonishment, a wounded R.F.A. man, sitting near, chimed in and said, "It's true, Sister ! We all saw it. First there was a sort of yellow mist, sort of rising out before the Germans as they came on to the top of the hill; come on like a solid wall they did——springing out of the earth, just solid ; no end of them. I just gave up. It's no use fighting the whole German race, thinks I. It's all up with us ! The next minute up comes this funny cloud of light, and when it clears off there's a tall man with yellow hair, in golden armour, on a *white* horse, holding his sword up, and his mouth open as if he was saying, ' Come on, boys !' . . . Then, before you could say ' Knife,' the Germans had turned, and we were after them, fighting like ninety. We had a few scores to settle, Sister, and we fairly settled them."

Miss Campbell also cites the case of three men of the Irish Guards, who were fatally wounded and had asked for the Holy Sacrament to be administered to them before their death, and who with their dying lips told precisely the same story to the aged priest to whom they made confession.

The Reverend A. A. Boddy, Vicar of All Saints, Monkwear-mouth (who did duty with the troops at the front for upwards of two months) in the course of an address delivered at an open-air meeting, reported in the *Sunderland Echo* (*August 16th,* 1914) related some interesting stories told him by soldiers regarding these supernatural experiences. This clergyman also told his audience of similar tales having been related to the sister of a gentle-man who had generously given up his house as a convalescent home for wounded soldiers. One of these stories told to this lady by one of these wounded men was to the effect that, on an occasion when the British were hard pressed, the figure of a gigantic angel with outstretched wings hovered in a luminous cloud between the English and the advancing German lines : and that the latter,

furnished by the newspapers, and in the many pamphlets now being published on this subject. These are merely so much sensational gossip, calculated to excite and feed the morbidly curious, without any attempt at any explanation of these remarkable occurrences.

I will, however, remark, *en passant*, that if the stories published in the *Evening News* (*one month after these tales began to be noised about the camps on both the Eastern and Western fronts of the war*) and if they "*had no foundation in fact of any kind or sort*," but were spun out of the inner consciousness of their Author's brain, then I say that a more daring and wicked thing was never before attempted in the way of sensational journalism in this country. And this, in itself constitutes a glaring Sign of the fearful Times in which we are now living! "It is a snare to a man who devoureth that which is holy, and after vows to make enquiry." "Whoso boasteth himself of a false gift is like clouds and wind without rain." (Proverbs xx., 25 : xxv., 14) : and it is a very dreadful thing to trifle with serious matters affecting the present welfare and the future destinies of mankind.

The number of persons in the British, French, Belgian, and Russian armies who have declared that they were eye-witnesses of these strange and unearthly manifestations, is, I have said, very great, and comprises men of every rank and temperament——from the highly-educated officer down to the humble, and often illiterate private. And it is safe to say that, under the fearful circumstances in which these men were placed——the horrors of a retreat (always depressing, and especially repugnant to British troops) before savage and vindictive enemies, employing barbarous and unheard of methods in the conduct of this war, and who were known, habitu- ally, and out of studied malice, to ignore all the customary usages of warfare ; the dreadful scenes of bloodshed, blazing towns, hamlets, and detached dwellings : the ruined and fleeing peasantry : the care of wounded and dying comrades; their own pitiable condition of fatigue, hunger, and privation, and the terrible state of the country throughout which they struggled under the precarious cover of rear-guard actions——*these heroic souls were not in a frame of mind conducive to the evolution of romantic thoughts or ideas on any subject whatsoever, much less in the concoction of deliberate falsehoods regarding subjects of a religious or spiritual nature !*

The *Universe* publishes a story told by an officer to the effect that he saw at the front an apparition of men armed with bows from which they discharged flights of arrows into the German host : and that afterwards, when talking to one of the German prisoners, the latter enquired as to the name of the officer mounted

12

on a *white* horse who led the British, and gave it as his opinion that he must have borne a charmed life, for although he was such a conspicuous object, and hundreds were firing at him, none of them had been able to hit him !

A terribly wounded Lancashire Fusilier asked Miss Phyllis Campbell (who for some months acted as nurse at one of the Hospitals at the Front) for a medal or picture of St. George. Puzzled at the strange request, Miss Campbell inquired whether he was a Roman Catholic. "No," the man replied, "I am a Wesleyan Methodist, and I want a picture or a medal of St. George because I have seen him on a *white* horse, leading the British at Vitry-le-François, when the Allies turned upon the Germans." Seeing Miss Camp- bell's look of astonishment, a wounded R.F.A. man, sitting near, chimed in and said, "It's true, Sister ! We all saw it. First there was a sort of yellow mist, sort of rising out before the Germans as they came on to the top of the hill; come on like a solid wall they did——springing out of the earth, just solid ; no end of them. I just gave up. It's no use fighting the whole German race, thinks I. It's all up with us ! The next minute up comes this funny cloud of light, and when it clears off there's a tall man with yellow hair, in golden armour, on a *white* horse, holding his sword up, and his mouth open as if he was saying, ' Come on, boys ! ' . . . Then, before you could say ' Knife,' the Germans had turned, and we were after them, fighting like ninety. We had a few scores to settle, Sister, and we fairly settled them."

Miss Campbell also cites the case of three men of the Irish Guards, who were fatally wounded and had asked for the Holy Sacrament to be administered to them before their death, and who with their dying lips told precisely the same story to the aged priest to whom they made confession.

The Reverend A. A. Boddy, Vicar of All Saints, Monkwear- mouth (who did duty with the troops at the front for upwards of two months) in the course of an address delivered at an open-air meeting, reported in the *Sunderland Echo* (*August 16th*, 1914) related some interesting stories told him by soldiers regarding these supernatural experiences. This clergyman also told his audience of similar tales having been related to the sister of a gentle- man who had generously given up his house as a convalescent home for wounded soldiers. One of these stories told to this lady by one of these wounded men was to the effect that, on an occasion when the British were hard pressed, the figure of a gigantic angel with outstretched wings hovered in a luminous cloud between the English and the advancing German lines : and that the latter,

13

paused for an instant, and then retired in confusion. This lady, happening to speak on the subject in the presence of some officers, and in the course of her remarks implying that she discredited the story, was addressed by a colonel with this assurance, "Young lady, the thing really happened. You need not be incredulous. I saw it myself!"

But, perhaps, the best known of these testimonies as to the angelic manifestations at Mons, is that which was contributed to the *Weekly Dispatch* by Miss Callow, Secretary to the Higher Thought Centre, South Kensington. Miss Callow wrote:—

"An officer has sent to one of the members of the Centre, a detailed account of a vision that appeared to himself and others when fighting against fearful odds at Mons. He plainly saw an apparition representing St. George, the patron saint of England, the exact counterpart of a picture that hangs to-day in a London Restaurant. So terrible was their plight at the time that the officer could not refrain from appealing to the vision to help them. Then, as if the enemy had seen the apparition, the Germans abandoned their positions in precipitate terror. In other instances men had written about seeing clouds of Celestial Horsemen hovering over the British lines."

A similar batch of stories comes from the Eastern theatre of war. Many of the Russian sentinels have stoutly maintained that they have seen Scobeloff, the hero of Plevna, in his conspicuous *white* uniform and mounted on his famous *white* charger, galloping in front of their lines and pointing westwards. This favourable omen to the cause of Russia is stated only to appear when the armies of the "Little Father" are in extraordinary straits, and it is confidently believed that the appearance of the ghost of the dashing general always means victory for the Russian armies, and confusion to her enemies.

"WHY SHOULD IT BE THOUGHT A THING INCREDIBLE WITH YOU."

(Acts xxvi., 8).

The Saviour said that amongst the other terrifying phenomena, which, in these days of godless apostacy, should startle mankind and cause "men's hearts to *fail* them for fear, and for looking after those things which are coming on the earth" for "the powers of heaven shall be shaken," " would be " *fearful* (or terrifying) *sights and great signs shall there be from heaven* " (Luke xxi., 11, 25 and 26). And, indeed, the whole prophetic record, in both the Old and New Testaments, teems with prognostications as to the dreadful character of the horrific " Signs of the Times " which shall precede the manifestation of the Antichrist, and close of this age, when " *your young men shall see visions, and your old men shall dream dreams. And I will shew wonders in the heavens and in the earth,* blood, and fire, and pillars of smoke. The sun shall be turned into darkness, and the moon into blood, before the great and terrible day of the Lord come." (Joel ii., 28-31).

Many prominent Clergymen and Ministers of nearly every Denomination have written or preached upon these " Visions of Angels " in Belgium, France, and elsewhere, conspicuous amongst whom are Bishop Welldon, Bishop Taylor Smith (Chaplain-General to the Forces), Dean Hensley Henson, Dr. Horton, at Manchester, The Rev. ——— Lancaster, at Weymouth, The Rev. A. A. Boddy, at Monkwearmouth, and Sir Joseph Compton Rickett, President of the Free Church Council. But, perhaps, the opinions of the Rev. Dinsdale T. Young, the venerable ex-President of the Wesleyan Conference, expressed to the Special Commission of the *Christian Globe*, and published by that evangelican organ in its issue of August 19th last, are the most valuable and inspiring to the devout believer in the Omnipotence and Omnipresence of God, the Merits of the Redeemer, and the teachings of the Holy Spirit, as revealed in the Scriptures which He has caused to be " written aforetime for our learning, that we through patience and comfort of the Scriptures might have hope " (Rom. xv., 4). I will here give some of the reverend gentleman's remarks,—with this proviso, that the subject had for him a peculiar interest, as he has a son just returned wounded from the Dardanelles :—

" I can't say anything as to the truth of the instances reported in the present war, but I emphatically believe in their possibility. I think that the mystical side of Christianity has been sadly ignored in these days, and what is falsely called the practical side has been allowed far too much to monopolise attention. I think mysticism is a practical fact in modern life, and I don't see how a believer in the Bible can reject it. I do say—without having any evidence as to these alleged interventions—that I most strongly believe in their possibility, and I do not doubt that they may have occurred. I go to Butler's famous argument from probability, and I think these happenings are highly probable.

" Why do I think so ? Because in the Bible there is a special

14

15

paused for an instant, and then retired in confusion. This lady, happening to speak on the subject in the presence of some officers, and in the course of her remarks implying that she discredited the story, was addressed by a colonel with this assurance, "Young lady, the thing really happened. You need not be incredulous. I saw it myself!"

But, perhaps, the best known of these testimonies as to the angelic manifestations at Mons, is that which was contributed to the *Weekly Dispatch* by Miss Callow, Secretary to the Higher Thought Centre, South Kensington. Miss Callow wrote:—

"An officer has sent to one of the members of the Centre, a detailed account of a vision that appeared to himself and others when fighting against fearful odds at Mons. He plainly saw an apparition representing St. George, the patron saint of England, the exact counterpart of a picture that hangs to-day in a London Restaurant. So terrible was their plight at the time that the officer could not refrain from appealing to the vision to help them. Then, as if the enemy had seen the apparition, the Germans abandoned their positions in precipitate terror. In other instances men had written about seeing clouds of Celestial Horsemen hovering over the British lines."

A similar batch of stories comes from the Eastern theatre of war. Many of the Russian sentinels have stoutly maintained that they have seen Scobeloff, the hero of Plevna, in his conspicuous *white* uniform and mounted on his famous *white* charger, galloping in front of their lines and pointing westwards. This favourable omen to the cause of Russia is stated only to appear when the armies of the "Little Father" are in extraordinary straits, and it is confidently believed that the appearance of the ghost of the dashing general always means victory for the Russian armies, and confusion to her enemies.

"WHY SHOULD IT BE THOUGHT A THING INCREDIBLE WITH YOU."

(Acts xxvi., 8).

The Saviour said that amongst the other terrifying phenomena, which, in these days of godless apostacy, should startle mankind and cause "men's hearts *to fail* them for fear, and for looking after those things which are coming on the earth " for " the powers of

heaven shall be shaken," " would be " *fearful* (or terrifying) *sights and great signs shall there be/from heaven* " (Luke xxi., 11, 25 and 26). And, indeed, the whole prophetic record, in both the Old and New Testaments teems with prognostications as to the dreadful character of the horrific " Signs of the Times " which shall precede the manifestation of the Antichrist, and close of this age, when " *your young men shall see visions, and your old men shall dream dreams. And I will shew wonders in the heavens and in the earth*, blood, and fire, and pillars of smoke. The sun shall be turned into darkness, and the moon into blood, before the great and terrible day of the Lord come." (Joel ii., 28-31).

Many prominent Clergymen and Ministers of nearly every Denomination have written or preached upon these " Visions of Angels" in Belgium, France, and elsewhere, conspicuous amongst whom are Bishop Welldon, Bishop Taylor Smith (Chaplain-General to the Forces), Dean Hensley Henson, Dr. Horton, at Manchester, The Rev. —— Lancaster, at Weymouth, The Rev. A. A. Boddy, at Monkwearmouth, and Sir Joseph Compton Rickett, President of the Free Church Council. But, perhaps, the opinions of the Rev. Dimsdale T. Young, the venerable ex-President of the Wesleyan Conference, expressed to the Special Commission of the *Christian Globe*, and published by that evangelican organ in its issue of August 19th last, are the most valuable and inspiring to the devout believer in the Omnipotence and Omnipresence of God, the Merits of the Redeemer, and the teachings of the Holy Spirit, as revealed in the Scriptures which He has caused to be " written aforetime for our learning, that we through patience and comfort of the Scriptures might have hope " (Rom. xv., 4). I will here give some of the reverend gentleman's remarks,—with this proviso, that the subject had for him a peculiar interest, as he has a son just returned wounded from the Dardanelles :—

" I can't say anything as to the truth of the instances reported in the present war, but I emphatically believe in their possibility. I think that the mystical side of Christianity has been sadly ignored in these days, and what is falsely called the practical side has been allowed far too much to monopolise attention. I think mysticism is a practical fact in modern life, and I don't see how a believer in the Bible can reject it. I do say—without having any evidence as to these alleged interventions—that I most strongly believe in their possibility, and I do not doubt that they may have occurred. I go to Butler's famous argument from probability, and I think these happenings are highly probable.

" Why do I think so? Because in the Bible there is a special that is a law universal, and I think it largely applies to these particular circumstances.

"I can give you practical proof of what I mean. I was very much impressed by seeing in the papers, a story, which is thoroughly well verified, of an officer who had charge out yonder, in France, of what may be called the Correspondence Bureau—that is he read the letters sent from and received by the men at the front. He had been an agnostic, but he said that the letters from the men who were Christians, and from their people who were Christians showed such support and comfort that it convinced him of the practical power of the Christian religion. After all, the argument from practical effect has always played a supreme part, both in the Bible and out of it.

"So I would not discourage anyone from believing in Divine Intervention, in fact, I should expect that there would be angelic interventions in this present time—whether the alleged ones have been interventions or not. I am convinced that there are such happenings, though I do not profess to explain them; it is of the essence of faith that it deals with the unseen. If I only believed in forces because I could discern them, then I am a very poor believer, indeed, to put it mildly.

"I wish more people in the Churches had a more bracing faith in the supernatural, because it is a contradiction for a Christian not to believe in it; the great vice, to my mind, in modern religion being its reluctance to accept the supernatural. That disbelief is the root-secret of the so-called German Higher Criticism—which, I may add, I trust this war will abolish. I am persuaded that there is bound to be a great revival of the old evangelical theology, and that is one of the good results we may expect from this terrible war. We shall get back our faith in the Bible and in the God of the Bible."

SCRIPTURAL REFERENCES TO DIRECT DIVINE INTERVENTION IN HUMAN AFFAIRS.

At the Passage of the Red Sea, by the Israelites during their Exodus from Egypt, we read, "*And the Angel of God, which went*

that is a law universal, and I think it largely applies to these particular circumstances.

"I can give you practical proof of what I mean. I was very much
impressed by seeing in the papers, a story, which is thoroughly
well verified, of an officer who had charge out yonder, in France,
of what may be called the Correspondence Bureau—that is he read
the letters sent from and received by the men at the front. He
had been an agnostic, but he said that the letters from the men
who were Christians, and from their people who were Christians
showed such support and comfort that it convinced him of the
practical power of the Christian religion. After all, the argument
from practical effect has always played a supreme part, both in the
Bible and out of it.

"So I would not discourage anyone from believing in Divine
Intervention, in fact, I should expect that there would be angelic
interventions in this present time—whether the alleged ones have
been interventions or not. I am convinced that there are such
happenings, though I do not profess to explain them; it is of the
essence of faith that it deals with the unseen. If I only believed
in forces because I could discern them, then I am a very poor believer, indeed, to put it mildly.

"I wish more people in the Churches had a more bracing faith
in the supernatural, because it is a contradiction for a Christian
not to believe in it; the great vice, to my mind, in modern religion
being its reluctance to accept the supernatural. That disbelief is
the root-secret of the so-called German Higher Criticism—which,
I may add, I trust this war will abolish. I am persuaded that
there is bound to be a great revival of the old evangelical theology,
and that is one of the good results we may expect from this terrible
war. We shall get back our faith in the Bible and in the God of
the Bible."

SCRIPTURAL REFERENCES TO DIRECT DIVINE INTERVENTION IN HUMAN AFFAIRS.

At the Passage of the Red Sea, by the Israelites during their
Exodus from Egypt, we read, " *And the Angel of God, which went*

Israel: and it was a cloud and darkness, but it gave light by night: so that the one came not near the other all the night. And it came to pass that in the morning watch, the Lord looked unto the host of the Egyptians through the pillar of fire and of the cloud, and troubled the host of the Egyptians" (Exodus xiv., 10, 20, 24).

This circumstance connected with Israel's deliverance from the very Pharaoh (one of whose monoliths, erroneously called "Cleopatra's Needle," now adorns the Thames' Embankment) is also alluded to by the Psalmist Asaph in the 78th Psalm, v., 49, "He cast upon them (the Egyptians) the fierceness of His anger, wrath, and indignation, and trouble, by sending evil angels among them."

"And it came to pass when Joshua was by Jericho, that he lifted up his eyes and looked, and behold there stood a Man over against him with His sword drawn in His Hand: and Joshua went unto Him, and said unto Him, 'Art Thou for us or for our adversaries?' And He said, 'Nay, but as Captain of the host of the Lord am I now come.' And Joshua fell on his face to the earth, and did worship, and said unto Him, 'What saith my Lord unto His servant?' And the Captain of the Lord's host said unto Joshua, 'Loose thy shoe from off thy foot: for the place whereon thou standest is holy.' And Joshua did so!" (Joshua v., 13-15).

This awful and mysterious Visitant to Israel's Leader, at a time of great anxiety and perplexity, Who received Joshua's worship and peremptorily ordered him to remove his shoes because the place was hallowed by His Presence, could have been no other than the Great Captain of our Salvation Himself,——"the Rock that followed them (the Israelites): and that Rock was Christ." Compare Revelation xix., 10: xxii., 8 and 9: Exodus iii., 5: Heb. ii., 10: 1 Corinthians x., 4. And I am of opinion that it was the invisible hands of "the Lord's host," under the immediate command of their Great Captain, which threw down the walls of Jericho, Israel's first conquest in Canaan.

"And it came to pass, as they (the Five Kings and their Armies at Gideon) fled from before Israel, and were in the going down to Beth-horon, that the Lord cast down great stones from heaven upon them unto Azekah, and they died: they were more which died with hailstones than they whom the Children of Israel slew with the sword. . . . For the Lord fought for Israel." (Joshua x., 11 and 14).

Deborah and Barak, in their exultant outburst of praise for the victory over the army of Jabin, commanded by the renowned Sisera, sang—"They fought from heaven: the stars in their courses fought against Sisera." (Judges v; 20-22).

In this book of Judges, we also find recorded the apparition of the Angel who rebuked the people at Bochim; the Angel who appeared to Gideon: and also the one who foretold the birth of Samson to the wondering parents of that hero. (Judges ii., 1: vi., 12: xiii., 3, 9-20).

There is no poetic exaggeration in the Poetry of the Holy Scriptures! Any person inclined to think so, would do well to compare the passages occurring in the 22nd Psalm and 53rd Chapter of Isaiah with the story of Christ's life on earth and His shameful death on Golgotha, and I feel sure that they will soon become disabused of this erroneous conception.

In the wonderful poetic portion of the Book of Job are many passages relating to celestial visitations. Thus Eliaphaz says, "In thoughts from the visions of the night, when deep sleep falleth upon man, fear came upon me and trembling, which made all my bones to shake. Then a spirit passed before my face: the hair of my flesh stood up. It stood still but I could not discern the form thereof: A form was before mine eyes: there was silence, and I heard a voice saying,——" (Job iv., 13-16).

When "Zarah the Ethiopian," (the Egyptian, Usarkon ii.) invaded Judah with 1,000,000 men, accompanied by 300 chariots the pious Asa prayed for succour, and we are told:—" So the Lord smote the Ethiopians before Asa, and before Judah: and the Ethiopians fled, and the Ethiopians could not recover themselves, for they were destroyed before the Lord, and before His host." (2 Chronicles xiv., 9-15).

When the Syrian (not Assyrian) army besieged Dothan in order to capture Elisha, the prophet's servant was in a great fright, and cried out, "Alas, my master! how shall we do?" The man of God answered, "Fear not; for they that be with us are more than they that be with them!"——" And Elisha prayed, and said, Lord, I pray Thee, open his eyes that he may see.' And the Lord opened the eyes of the young man, and he saw: and behold, the mountain was full of horses and chariots of fire round about Elisha." (2 Kings vi., 15-17).

At the siege of Samaria, the overwhelming Syrian army simply bolted: "For the Lord had made the host of the Syrians to hear a noise of chariots, and a noise of horses, even the noise of a great host: and they said one to another,' Lo, the King of Israel hath hired against us the Kings of the Hittites and the Kings of the Egyptians, to come upon us. Wherefore they arose and fled in the twilight, and left their tents, and their horses, and their asses, even the camp as it was, and fled for their life. . . . They took therefore two chariot horses:

18   19

Israel : and it was a cloud and darkness, but it gave light by night : so that the one came not near the other all the night. And it came to pass that in the morning watch, the Lord looked unto the host of the Egyptians through the pillar of fire and of the cloud, and troubled the host of the Egyptians " (Exodus xiv., 19, 20, 24).

This circumstance connected with Israel's deliverance from the very Pharaoh (one of whose monoliths, erroneously called "Cleopatra's Needle," now adorns the Thames' Embankment) is also alluded to by the Psalmist Asaph in the 78th Psalm, v., 49, " He cast upon them (the Egyptians) the fierceness of His anger, wrath, and indignation, and trouble, by sending evil angels among them."

" And it came to pass when Joshua was by Jericho, that he lifted up his eyes and looked, and behold there stood a Man over against him with His sword drawn in His Hand : and Joshua went unto Him, and said unto Him, ' Art Thou for us or for our adversaries ?' And He said, ' Nay, but as Captain of the host of the Lord am I now come.' And Joshua fell on his face to the earth, and did worship, and said unto Him, ' What saith my Lord unto His servant ? ' And the Captain of the Lord's host said unto Joshua, ' Loose thy shoe from off thy foot : for the place whereon thou standest is holy.' And Joshua did so !" (Joshua v., 13-15).

This awful and mysterious Visitant to Israel's Leader, at a time of great anxiety and perplexity, Who received Joshua's worship and peremptorily ordered him to remove his shoes because the place was hallowed by His Presence, could have been no other than the Great Captain of our Salvation Himself,——'the Rock that followed them (the Israelites) : and that Rock was Christ." Compare Revelation xix., 10 : xxii., 8 and 9 : Exodus iii., 5 : Heb. ii., 10 : 1 Corinthians x., 4. And I am of opinion that it was the invisible hands of "the Lord's host," under the immediate command of their Great Captain, which threw down the walls of Jericho, Israel's first conquest in Canaan.

And it came to pass, as they (the Five Kings and their Armies at Gideon) fled from before Israel, and were in the going down to Beth-horon, that the Lord cast down great stones from heaven upon them unto Azekah, and they died : they were more which died with hailstones than they whom the Children of Israel slew with the sword. . . . For the Lord fought for Israel." (Joshua x., 11 and 14).

Deborah and Barak, in their exultant outburst of praise for the victory over the army of Jabin, commanded by the renowned Sisera, song—" They fought from heaven : the stars in their courses fought against Sisera." (Judges v., 20-22).

18

In this book of Judges, we also find recorded the apparition of the Angel who rebuked the people at Bochim : the Angel who appeared to Gideon : and also the one who foretold the birth of Samson to the wondering parents of that hero. (Judges ii., 1 : vi., 12 : xiii., 3, 9-20).

There is no poetic exaggeration in the Poetry of the Holy Scriptures ! Any person inclined to think so, would do well to compare the passages occurring in the 22nd Psalm and 53rd Chapter of Isaiah with the story of Christ's life on earth and His shameful death on Golgotha, and I feel sure that they will soon become disabused of this erroneous conception.

In the wonderful poetic portion of the Book of Job are many passages relating to celestial visitations. Thus Eliphaz says, " In thoughts from the visions of the night, when deep sleep falleth upon man, fear came upon me and trembling, which made all my bones to shake. Then a spirit passed before my face : the hair of my flesh stood up. It stood still but I could not discern the form thereof : A form was before mine eyes : there was silence, and I heard a voice saying.——" (Job iv., 13-16).

When " Zarah the Ethiopian," (the Egyptian, Usarkon ii.) invaded Judah with 1,000,000 men, accompanied by 300 chariots the pious Asa prayed for succour, and we are told :—" So the Lord smote the Ethiopians before Asa, and before Judah : and the Ethiopians fled.   .   .   and the Ethiopians could not recover themselves, for they were destroyed before the Lord, and before His host." (2 Chronicles xiv., 9-15).

When the Syrian (not Assyrian) army besieged Dothan in order to capture Elisha, the prophet's servant was in a great fright, and cried out, " Alas, my master ! how shall we do ? " The man of God answered, "Fear not ; for they that be with us are more than they that be with them !"——" And Elisha prayed, and said, ' Lord, I pray Thee, open his eyes that he may see.' And the Lord opened the eyes of the young man, and he saw : and behold, the mountain was full of horses and chariots of fire round about Elisha." (2 Kings vi., 15-17).

At the siege of Samaria, the overwhelming Syrian army simply bolted : " For the Lord had made the host of the Syrians to hear a noise of chariots, and a noise of horses, even the noise of a great host : and they said one to another,' Lo, the King of Israel hath hired against us the Kings of the Hittites and the Kings of the Egyptians, to come upon us.' Wherefore they arose and fled in the twilight, and left their tents, and their horses, and their asses, even the camp as it was, and fled for their life.   .   .   .   They took therefore two chariot horses :

19

and the King: and after the death of the Syrian, saying: "Go and cut off garments and vessels, which the Syrians had cast away on their backs. And the messengers returned and told the King." (2 Kings vii. 6, 7; and 1 M. 10.)

A modern parallel to this stampede of the Syrian Army is to be found in the wild game of Balilk Bom, when the entire Federal Army fled, paralised, on a mere rumour, that the Confederated forces were all coming to attack them. This Northern Army rushed away without even seeing the enemy!!

When Sennacherib (Sen-Aherib), the son and successor of Sargon, "the Great King (the King of Assyria)" invaded Judah, and sent "the Tartan (Commander-in-chief), Rab-Saris (Grand Master of the Eunuchs), and Rab-Shakeh (Chamberlain or Cup-bearer) with a great army unto Jerusalem," he forwarded a blasphemous letter to King Hezekiah, who at that moment devoutly took it to "God's House, and "spread it before the Lord." The answer to this humble and devout action was speedily given: "Thus saith the Lord, the God of Israel, whereas thou hast prayed to Me against Sennacherib King of Assyria, I have heard thee. He shall not come unto this city, nor shoot an arrow there, nor... before it, nor cast a mount against it. By the way that he came, by the same shall he return, and shall not come unto this city, saith the Lord. For I will defend this city, to save it, for Mine Own sake, and for My servant David's sake. And it came to pass that night, that the angel of the Lord went forth, and smote in the camp of the Assyrians an hundred fourscore and five thousand; and when men rose early in the morning behold they were all dead corpses." (2 Kings xvii, 17; xviii, 19, 20, 32, 35; R.V.)

The other instances of Angelic Visitations and Visions, scattered throughout the Old Testament, are too numerous for detailed specification. They form a large feature in the Books of Daniel, Ezekiel, and Zechariah, and are mainly prophetic in character. Some of these predictions have been already fulfilled; but the greater bulk refer to this generation which will see "the Son of Man coming in His Kingdom." (Matt. xvi, 28.)

VICTORY OF JUDAS MACCABEUS

In the 2nd Book of Maccabees (in the Apocryphal chapters, 8-10) we are told that Judas Maccabeus gained a notable victory over Lysias, the general of the armies of Antiochus Epiphanes, through

spiritual aid. The Syrian forces numbered 80,000 men; that of the Jews, 10,000 only. The writer says: When they (the Jews) were at Jerusalem, there appeared before them on horseback One in white apparel shaking his armour of gold. Then they marched forward in their armour; for the Lord was merciful to them.

ANGELIC VISITS AND VISIONS RECORDED IN THE NEW TESTAMENT

In this part of Holy Writ, we have recorded the Visits of the Angel Gabriel to Zecharias, in the Temple, to Mary, announcing the coming of the Redeemer; the appearance of Moses and Elijah, on the Mount of the Transfiguration, the Heavenly Voices at Christ's Baptism, in the holy mount, and when preaching during His last visit to Jerusalem; the Angels of the Resurrection, and those who appeared to the sorrowing disciples at the Ascension; the deliverance of the Apostles from prison by an Angel, Peter's deliverance by the same agency; and the apparition of the Man of Macedonia, crying, Come over into Macedonia and help us. See Luke i., 11, 26-29; Mark ix, 4-7; 2 Peter i, 17 and 18; Matt. iii, 17; John xii, 28; Matt. xxvii., 2, 7; Luke xxiv., 4-7; Acts i, 10 and 11; v., 19; xii., 7; xvi., 9.

The wonderful predictions of the three Apostles, Peter, Paul, John, and Jude, regarding the great and General Apostacy of these latter days, we now being dealt with in a remarkable Series of Articles on the Fulfilment of Holy Writ, which commenced on April 1st of this year, and are still running. These will amply repay perusal. Of the marvellous visions of John's Apocalypse, descriptive and prophetic, some have been fulfilled, some are now in course of fulfilment, but most relate to the near future — the new terribly near future!

PORTENTIOUS VISIONS BEFORE THE FALL OF JERUSALEM

As this tremendous event, in A.D. 70 — of great importance in the sight of Him by Whom? All the inhabitants are counted as nothing. Who doeth according to His Will in the army of heaven, and among the inhabitants of the earth, and none can stay His Hand

and the King sent after the host of the Syrians, saying ' Go and see.' And they went after them to Jordan ; and, lo, all the way was full of garments and vessels, which the Syrians had cast away in their haste. And the messengers returned and told the King." (2 Kings vii., 6, 7, and 14, 15).

A modern parallel to this stampede of the Syrian Army, is to be found in the wild panic of Bulls' Run, when the entire Federal Army fled, pell-mell, on a mere rumour that the Confederate Forces were advancing to the attack. This Northern Army rushed away without even seeing the enemy !

When Sennacherib (Sinn-akka-srba, the son and successor of Sargon) " the Great King, the King of Assyria," invaded Judah, and sent " the Tartan (Commander-in-chief), Rab-Saris (Grand Master of the Eunuchs), and Rab-Shakeh (Chamberlain or Cup-bearer) with a great army unto Jerusalem," he forwarded a blasphemous letter to King Hezekiah, which that monarch wisely took to God's House, and " spread before the Lord." The answer to this humble and devout action was speedily given. " *Thus saith the Lord, the God of Israel, whereas thou hast prayed to Me against Sennacherib, King of Assyria, I have heard thee.* . . . *He shall not come unto this city, nor shoot an arrow there, neither shall he come before it with shield, nor cast a mount against it. By the way that he came, by the same shall he return, and shall not come unto this city, saith the Lord. For I will defend this city, to save it, for Mine Own sake, and for My servant David's sake. And it came to pass that night, that the angel of the Lord went forth, and smote in the camp of the Assyrians an hundred, four score and five thousand ; and when men rose early in the morning, behold they were all dead corpses ! "* (2 Kings xviii., 17 : xix., 14, 20, 32—35. R.V.).

The other instances of Angelic Visitations and Visions, scattered throughout the Old Testament, are too numerous for detailed specification. They form a large feature in the Books of Daniel, Ezekiel, and Zechariah, and are mainly prophetic in character. Some of these predictions have been already fulfilled, but the great bulk refer to this generation which will see " the Son of Man coming in His Kingdom." (Matt. xvi., 28).

VICTORY OF JUDAS MACCABEUS.

In the 2nd Book of Maccabees (in the *Apocrypha*) chapter xi., 8-10. we are told that Judas Maccabeus gained a notable victory over Lysias, the general of the atrocious Antiochus Epiphanes, through

spiritual aid. The Syrian forces numbered 80,000 men ; that of the Jews, 10,000 only. The writer says " When they (the Jews) were at Jerusalem, there appeared before them on horseback One in *white* apparel shaking his armour of gold. Thus they marched forward in their armour ; for the Lord was merciful to them."

ANGELIC VISITS AND VISIONS RECORDED IN THE NEW TESTAMENT.

In this part of Holy Writ, we have recorded the Visits of the Angel Gabriel to Zecharias, in the Temple ; to Mary, announcing the coming of the Redeemer ; the appearance of Moses and Elijah, on the Mount of the Transfiguration ; the Heavenly Voices at Christ's Baptism ; "in the holy mount," and when preaching during His last visit to Jerusalem ; the Angels of the Resurrection, and those who appeared to the sorrowing disciples at the Ascension : the deliverance of the Apostles from prison by an Angel; Peter's deliverance by the same agency ; and the apparition of the Man of Macedonia, crying, " Come over into Macedonia and help us." See Luke i., 11, 26-29 : Mark ix., 4-7 : 2 Peter i., 17 and 18 : Matt. iii., 17 : John xii., 28 : Matt. xxviii., 2, 7 : Luke xxiv., 4-7 : Acts i., 10 and 11 : v., 19 : xii., 7 : xvi., 9.

The wonderful predictions of the three Apostles, Peter, Paul John, and Jude, regarding the great and General Apostacy of these latter days, are now being dealt with in a remarkable Series of Articles on the " Fulfilment of Holy Writ," which commenced on April 1st of this year, and are still running. These will amply repay perusal Of the marvellous visions of John's Apocalypse, descriptive and prophetic, some have been fulfilled, some are now in course of fulfilment, but most relate to the near future——the now terribly near future !

PORTENTIOUS VISIONS BEFORE THE FALL OF JERUSALEM.

As this tremendous event, in A.D. 70.——of great importance in the sight of Him by Whom " All the inhabitants are reputed as nothing," : Who " doeth according to His Will in the army of heaven and among the inhabitants of the earth ; and none can stay His Han or say unto Him, ' What doest Thou ? ' " (Daniel iv., 36) : and of tremendous effect in the destinies of God's chosen race, who since that time have been wanderers and vagabonds on the earth—— constituted one of the great Epochs in the world's history, we should expect that this high significance would be marked by some startling phenomena;—and such unquestionably was the case. Many are the wonderful stories related by Josephus (who accompanied Titus and was an eye-witness of repute of all that had occurred immediately before, during, and after the siege and fall of Jerusalem), but none of these are so remarkable as the prodigies seen in the fearful sights shown in the heavens. The Jewish Historian tells us that for a whole year a luminous Sword of gigantic size floated over the city ; and that for some months before the arrival of the Roman army before the city, Bodies of Soldiers in battle array were observed in the clouds both during the day and night, the latter apparitions being the most terrifying. But these alarming portents, so far from inducing the misguided Jews to repentance and reformation, only served to harden their hearts and stiffen their necks, until the Roman Armies, under Vespasian and Titus, appeared on the scene, and took away their place and nation.

LATER APPARITIONS FORETELLING THE FUTURE.

These all appear *to be of the nature of portents* ; and nearly all of them were significant of events which ultimately came to pass. And as if to knock the bottom out of the materialistic argument as to " psychic exaltation " and other metaphysical rubbish, (put forward by persons who could not recognise the human brain if shown to them on a dish, much less understand its various parts and their intricate and marvellous conformation, composition, and properties), these visions were vouchsafed to men in full possession of their faculties at the time of their appearance, and of a class not given to form fantastic anticipations as to the future. And, in my opinion, the late apparitions at Mons, and other parts of France and Belgium fall into the same category.

I find that I have only space in which to notice four of these phenomena :—The apparitions seen on Edge Hill, Warwick-shire, just after the Battle of Edge Hill, and significant of *the ultimate victory of the Parliamentary Forces later on at Naseby* : those of 1686, near Lanark, indicating the fate of *James II's Cam-*

or say unto Him, ' What doest Thou ? ' " (Daniel iv., 35) ; and of tremendous effect in the destinies of God's chosen race, who since that time have been wanderers and vagabonds on the earth—— constituted one of the great Epochs in the world's history, we should expect that this high significance would be marked by some startling phenomena;—and such unquestionably was the case. Many are the wonderful stories related by Josephus (who accompanied Titus and was an eye-witness of repute of all that had occurred immediately before, during, and after the siege and fall of Jerusalem), but none of these are so remarkable as the prodigies seen in the fearful sights shown in the heavens. The Jewish Historian tells us that for a whole year a luminous Sword of gigantic size floated over the city : and that for some months before the arrival of the Roman army before the city, Bodies of Soldiers in battle array were observed in the clouds both during the day and night, the latter apparitions being the most terrifying. But these alarming portents , so far from inducing the misguided Jews to repentance and reformation, only served to harden their hearts and stiffen their necks, until the Roman Armies, under Vespasian and Titus, appeared on the scene, and took away their place and nation.

LATER APPARITIONS FORETELLING THE FUTURE.

These all appear *to be of the nature of portents* ; and nearly all of them were significant of events which ultimately came to pass. And as if to knock the bottom out of the materialistic argument as to " psychic exaltation " and other metaphysical rubbish, (put forward by persons who could not recognise the human brain if shown to them on a dish, much less understand its various parts and their intricate and marvellous conformation, composition, and properties), these visions were vouchsafed to men in full possession of their faculties at the time of their appearance, and of a class not given to form fantastic anticipations as to the future. And, in my opinion, the late apparitions at Mons, and other parts of France and Belgium fall into the same category.

I find that I have only space in which to notice four of these phenomena :—The apparitions seen on Edge Hill, Warwickshire, just after the Battle of Edge Hill, and significant of *the ultimate victory of the Parliamentary Forces later on at Naseby* : those of 1686, near Lanark, indicating the fate of *James II's Cam-*

23

to their ears and eyes : runne awie they durst not, for feare of being made a prey to these infernall Souldiers, and so they, with muche feare and affright stayed to beholde the successe of the businesse, whiche at last suited to this effects : after some Three Hours fighte, that Army which carryed the King's Colours withdrew, or rather appeared to flie : the other remaining, as it were, masters of the fields. stayed a goode space triumphing, and expressing all the signes of joy and conqueste, and thenne, with all their drummes, trumpets, ordinance, and Shouldiers vanished: the poore menne were gladd they were gonne, that had so long staid them there against their wills, made with all haste to Kineton, and there knocking up Mr. Wood, a Justice of Peace, who called up his neighbour, Mr. Marshall, the Minister, they gave them an accounte of the whole passage, and averred it upon their Oathes to be true. At which affirmation of their being muche amazed, they shoulde hardlie have given credit to it, but woulde have conjectured to have been either madde or drunk, had they knot known some of them to have beene of approved integritie : and soe, suspending their judgements till the next night about the same houre, they, with some of the menne, and all the substantiall inhabitants of that and the neighbouring parishes, drew thither : where, about halfe-an-houre after their arrivall, on Sunday, being Christmas night appeared in the same tumultuous war-like manner the same two adverse Armies, fighting with so muche spite and spleen as formerly. The next night they appeared not, nor all the weeke, soe that the dwellers thereabout were in good hope that they hadde for ever departed : but on the ensuing Saturday Night, in the same place, and at the same houre, they were again seene with far greater tumult, fighting in the manner aforementioned for foure hours, and then vanished, appearing again on Sunday Night, and performing the same actions of hostilitie and bloodshed : soe that Mr. Wood and others whose faithe, it shoulde seeme, was not strong enough to carry them out against these delusions, forsook their habitations thereabout, and retired themselves to other and more secure dwellings; but Mr. Marshall staid and some others : and soe successively the next Saturday and Sunday the same tumults and prodigious sights were put in the state and condition they were formerlie. The rumour whereof coming to his Majestie at Oxford, he immediately dispatched thither Colonell Lewis Kirke, Captaine Dudley, Captaine Wainman, and three other gentlemenne of credit, to take full view and notice of the said businesse, who, first hearing the true attestations and relation of Mr. Marshall and others staid there till the Saturday night following, wherin they hearde and saw the foresaid prodiges, and soe on Sunday, distinctly knowing divers of the apparitions or incorporeall substances by their faces, as that

14

to their ears and eyes: runne awie they durst not, for feare of being made a prey to these infernall Souldiers, and so they, with muche feare and affright stayed to beholde the successe of the businesse, whiche at last suited to this effecte: after some Three Hours fighte, that Army which carryed the King's Colours withdrew, or rather appeared to flie: the other remaining, as it were, masters of the fields. stayed a goode space triumphing, and expressing all the signes of joy and conqueste, and thenne, with all their drummes, trumpets, ordinance, and Shouldiers vanished: the poore menne were gladd they were gonne, that had so long staid them there against their wills, made with all haste to Kineton, and there knocking up Mr. Wood, a Justice of Peace, who called up his neighbour, Mr. Marshall, the Minister, they gave them an accounte of the whole passage, and averred it upon their Oathes to be true. At which affirmation of their being muche amazed, they shoulde hardlie have given credit to it, but woulde have conjectured to have been either madde or drunk, had they knot known some of them to have beene of approved integritie: and soe, suspending their judgements till the next night about the same houre, they, with some of the menne, and all the substantiall inhabitants of that and the neighbouring parishes, drew thither: where, about halfe-an-houre after their arrivall, on Sunday, being Christmas night appeared in the same tumultuous war-like manner the same two adverse Armies, fighting with so muche spite and spleen as formerly. The next night they appeared not, nor all the weeke, soe that the dwellers thereabout were in good hope that they hadde for ever departed: but on the ensuing Saturday Night, in the same place, and at the same houre, they were again scene with far greater tumull, fighting in the manner afore-mentioned for foure houres, and then vanished, appearing again on Sunday Night, and performing the same actions of hostilitie and bloodshed: soe that Mr. Wood and others whose faithe, it shoulde seeme, was not strong enough to carry them out against these delusions, forsook their habitations thereabout, and retired themselves to other and more secure dwellings; but Mr. Marshall staid and some others: and soe successively the next Saturday and Sunday the same tumults and prodigious sights were put in the state and condition they were formerlie. The rumour whereof coming to his Majestie at Oxford, he immediately dispatched thither Colonell Lewis Kirke, Captaine Dudley, Captaine Wainman, and three other gentlemenne of credit, to take full view and notice of the said businesse, who, first hearing the true attestations and relation of Mr. Marshall and others staid there till the Saturday night following, wherin they hearde and saw the fore-mentioned prodiges, and soe on Sunday, distinctly knowing divers of the apparitions or incorporeall substances by their faces, as that

24

had not the slightest doubt but that they were substantial forms of flesh and blood. They counted at least sixteen pairs of columns, and had abundance of time to observe every particular. Marching in the distance they could descry some Highlanders, who apparently sought to escape from the troops they beheld in front of them; and they could distinguish some of the tartans. The front ranks marched seven abreast : the men were clothed in red, and their arms shone brightly in the sun. In the midst of them was an animal of some kind, which the soldiers drove furiously before them with their bayonets. The younger of the two spectators observed to his father that every now and then the rear ranks were obliged to run in order to overtake the van : and the elder, who had served as a soldier, remarked, that that was always the case, and recommended him, if ever he enlisted as a soldier, always to try and march in the front. There was only one mounted officer, and he rode an iron-grey dragoon horse, wore a gold-laced hat, blue Huzzar cloak, with wide open sleeves lined with red. The two men observed him in particular, and said he should recognise him anywhere. They were afraid of being observed, and perhaps forced to go along with the troops : and whilst climbing over a dyke to get out of the way the whole thing vanished.

Telling their tale in Inverness——long before Charles Edward Stuart had appeared in Scotland——both father and son were brought before the bailiff, or magistrate, who, on hearing the re-cital, advised the worthy farmer to " Gang awa, mon, and pit a drap mair watter in it next time ! " Yet in little more than a year's time, that same officer,——the Duke of Cumberland,—— wearing the gold-laced hat, and mounted on the iron-grey dragoon horse, led his forces into the town of Inverness !

FORESHADOWINGS OF CAMPAIGNS OF 1813-14, AND OF WATERLOO, AT RIPLEY, IN 1812.

Several bands of Visionary Troops were seen in Havanah Park, near Ripley, by a substantial farmer, named Jackson, and a lad of fifteen, called Turner, in April, 1812, before Napeolon started on his ill-fated Russian Campaign, and prior to the Campaigns of 1813 and '14 and that of Belgium, was even dreamt of. First large bodies of troops clad in dark-blue uniforms were seen retreating before other troops, some of whom were in white, some dark grey, and some in

POSTSCRIPT.

Although the " Fingers of a man's hand have come forth and written over against the candlestick upon the plaister of the wall," and notwithstanding that " the vision " has been made so plain " that he may run that readeth it," and " wayfaring men, though fools, cannot err " as to its fearful import, yet the bulk of this nation, and the vast majority of mankind, cannot see " the part of the hand that wrote " ; and still continue to rush madly along " the broadway that leadeth to destruction." This behaviour is just what the Holy Scripture has predicted would be the case in these latter days ! (Dan., v., 5 : Habak. ii , 2 ; Isaiah xxxv., 8 : Matt. vii., 13).

I would most earnestly ask my readers to divert their attention from Western Europe and look towards *Mesopotamia*—" the land of Shinar " (Gen. x., 10 : xi., 1), *Palestine*, and *Egypt*, for *it is in these regions of the earth that the great closing scenes of the world-drama now opening, will be enacted* ! (Isaiah xix., 23-25). Europe (except so far as the House of Israel is concerned), is counted as a " very little thing " in the Eyes of Him with Whom " All the inhabitants of the earth are reputed as nothing " : Who " doeth according to His Will in the army of heaven, and among the inhabitants of the earth : and none can stay His Hand, or say unto Him, ' What doest Thou ? ' " (Isaiah xl., 15 : Dan. iv., 35). Europe is of small account in the sight of God !

I would also urge the necessity of closely observing the movements of that Dano-Russian-Hohenzollern Family, now on the Throne of Greece, for out of this Family will arise One that will become " a mighty one upon the earth," the " King of fierce countenance and understanding dark sentences," to whom all the monarchs of the earth will bow, and all those " whose names are *not* written in the Book of Life, will worship as "The Great Power of God." (Gen. x., 8 : Dan. viii., 23 : Rev. xiii., 8 : Acts viii., 10). ——Satan's Masterpiece, the **Pseudo-Messiah**, or **Antichrist** !

28

POSTSCRIPT.

Although the " Fingers of a man's hand have come forth and
written over against the candlestick upon the plaister of the wall,"
and notwithstanding that " the vision " has been made so plain
" that he may run that readeth it," and " wayfaring men, though
fools, cannot err " as to its fearful import, yet the bulk of this
nation, and the vast majority of mankind, cannot see " the part
of the hand that wrote " ; and still continue to rush madly along
" the broadway that leadeth to destruction." This behaviour is just
what the Holy Scripture has predicted would be the case in these
latter days ! (Dan., v., 5 : Habak. ii. ,2 ; Isaiah xxxv., 8 : Matt.
vii., 13).

I would most earnestly ask my readers to divert their attention
from Western Europe and look towards *Mesopotamia*—" the land
of Shinar " (Gen. x., 10 : xi., 1), *Palestine*, and *Egypt*, for *it is in
these regions of the earth that the great closing scenes of the world-
drama now opening, will be enacted* ! (Isaiah xix., 23-25). Europe
(except so far as the House of Israel is concerned), is counted
as a " very little thing " in the Eyes of Him with Whom ' All the
inhabitants of the earth are reputed as 'nothing " : Who " doeth
according to His Will in the army of heaven, and among the inhabitants of the earth : and none can stay His Hand, or say unto
Him, ' What doest Thou ? ' " (Isaiah xl., 15 : Dan. iv., 35). Europe
is of small account in the sight of God !

I would also urge the necessity of closely observing the movements of that Dano-Russian-Hohenzollern Family, now on the
Throne of Greece, for out of this Family will arise One that will
become " a mighty one upon the earth," the " King of fierce
countenance and understanding dark sentences," to whom all the
monarchs of the earth will bow, and all those " whose names are
not written in the Book of Life, will worship as "The Great Power
of God." (Gen. x., 8 : Dan. viii., 23 : Rev. xiii., 8 : Acts viii., 10).
——Satan's Masterpiece. the **Pseudo-Messiah**, or **Antichrist** !

" For I know that my Redeemer liveth, and that He shall stand up at the latter day upon the earth ! and though after my skin worms destroy this body, yet without my flesh shall I see God ! Whom I shall see on my side, and not as a stranger.". (Job xix., 25-27.

Psalms xxiii : xxvii : xlvi : lxxiii : xci : xcvi : c : civ : cvii : cxvi : cxxi : cxlv : cxlvii : Isaiah xxxv :

Psalm iv., 7 and 8 : v., 12 : vi., 9 : ix., 17 : xvii., 15; xxix. 11 : xxxi., 2, : xxxix., 17 and 18.

Isaiah xxxviii., 16 and 17 : xl., 25, 26, 27 - 31 : xli., 10 : xliii., 2, 7, 25, 26 : xlix., 15, 16 : lii., 11 and 12 : liv., 17 : lix., 1 : lxi, 10 : lxv., 24 : lxvi., 1 and 2, and 13.

Daniel, xii., 3 : Micah vii., 18 and 19 : Habak., iii 17 and 18 : Malachi iii., 16 -18.

" Behold wh it manner of love the Father hath bestowed upon us that we should be calle'l the sons of God. . . Beloved, now are we the sons of God, and it doth not yet appear what we shall be; but we know that, when He shall appear, we shall be like Him, for we shall see Him as He is " (1 John iii., 1 and 2). ". As we have borne the image of the earthly, we shall also bear the image of the heavenly." (1 Cor. xv., 49).

" Giving thanks unto the Father, Who hath made us meet to be partakers of the inheritance of the saints in light : Who hath delivered us from the power of darkness, and hath translated us into the Kingdom of His Dear Son"(Coloss. i., 12 and 13). "Who shall change our vile body that it may be fashioned like unto His Glorious Body, according to His mighty working whereby He is able to subdue all things unto Himself." (Philip iii., 21).

" A Crown of Righteousness. . . . unto all that love His appearing " (2 Tim. iv., 8). " An inheritance incorruptible, and undefiled, and that fadeth not away, reserved in heaven for you " (1 Peter i., 4). " There remaineth, therefore, a rest for the people of God " (Heb. iv., 9).

" If God be for us, who can be against us ? " " Who shall separate us from the Love of Christ ? Shall tribulation, or distress, or persecution, or famine, or nakedness, or peril, or sword ? Nay in all these things we are more than conquerors through Him that loved us ! Death is swallowed up in Victory ! O Death, where is thy sting ? O Grave, where is thy Victory ? But thanks be to God, Who giveth us the Victory through our Lord Jesus Christ ! ! ! " (Rom. viii., 31, 35 and 37 : 1 Cor. xv., 54, 55 and 57).

"THE FULFILMENT OF HOLY WRIT"

¶ *Especially in regard to the tremendous happenings of to-day.*

IS now being dealt with by a ripe Biblical Scholar in a remarkable Series of Articles, now appearing in the

CHRISTIAN GLOBE,

Published every Thursday, *One Penny*. Of all News Agents, or at any of Messrs. W. H. Smith & Sons' Bookstalls.

CPSIA information can be obtained
at www.ICGtesting.com
Printed in the USA
BVHW041444111218
535331BV00020B/886/P

9 780259 420583